A souvenir guide

Powis Castle Garden

Powys

National Trust

A Multi-layered Garden

Wales is famous for its rugged landscapes and ancient fortresses and less known for its gardens, and yet Powis Castle has one of the finest gardens in Britain. Visitors come from all over the world to enjoy its superb horticultural craftsmanship and its rich history.

Perched on a rocky ridge, Powis Castle is a real fortified medieval castle, complete with drum towers and massively thick stone walls. Later, less violent centuries saw the castle transformed into a palace, its towering walls opened up with tall windows to illuminate sumptuous interiors.

Below those windows, gardens were made which, far from being rustic, small-town attempts, were the height of international fashion. If the garden today seems a delightful surprise here in deepest Wales, how much more amazing must it have seemed in the past.

Above View from the Top
Terrace in autumn

Left The Top Terrace

Slices of history

Many a great garden can show only its most
recent developments, because it has been
created over the remains of older gardens,
each layer loved in its day but now buried
under the tide of fashion.

The wonder of Powis Castle is that it has
retained most of its historic styles; its
Italianate terraces, its wooded landscape
garden on the Wilderness ridge, its opulent
Edwardian Formal Garden. All are still here
and thriving, now enriched by the last
100 years of plantsmanship and
skilled gardening.

Formal beginnings

The garden we see today has its origins in the
1680s, when William Herbert, 1st Marquess of
Powis (c.1626–96) employed architect William
Winde to develop a series of terraces and
formal grass slopes against the south-facing
ridge below the Castle. Winde had made a
similar garden at Cliveden, Buckinghamshire,
in the 1660s and was at this time working on
Powis's interiors.

Theatrical terraces

Some of Powis's terraces are as much as 20m deep
and to create them it was necessary to blast out
the bare rock, build up retaining walls and bring in
huge quantities of soil. At the centre point of the
main terraces lay an aviary, an orangery, and open
spaces for social use, decorated with lead
statuary, urns and balustrades.

Below the upper, more formal terraces,
crisp-edged grass banks continued the
descent to the level land below and parallel
flights of steps allowed one to descend in
grandeur from top to bottom.

Surprising sight

In those early days the Castle was approached
from the east (today you will enter it from the
west) and as one stepped up to the great
classical portico and upper terrace on arrival,
suddenly one could look down upon the whole
of the terrace garden below. It was in effect a
secret valley of sophisticated ornamental
gardening, hidden from the south and west by
a wooded ridge, to the east by tall trees, and to
the north by the Castle itself.

The Dutch influence

In 1688 the 1st Marquess, a Catholic, fled to France with the exiled King James II and died there. His new garden in Wales lay uncompleted until his son the 2nd Marquess (*c.*1665–1745) returned to Britain in 1703 and began to work on the garden once more, this time with the help of Adrian Duval, a French gardener then working in Holland.

On the flat land at the foot of the terraces a water garden or Pleasure Ground in the Dutch style was created, of flat grass plats (areas) decorated with sculpture, and with pools and a grand cascade and basin. The water garden covered as much land as the Castle and terraces combined.

It was possible then to stand upon the ridge above the cascade and gaze across a Dutch water garden to the Italian Renaissance-style terraces and above these to the ancient Castle backed by its medieval deer park. Ancient stood above modern in spectacular formal progression.

Above *View of Powis Castle, Powys, seen across the Great Lawn* by Samuel and Nathaniel Buck, 1742

Right Formal hedges and 18th-century lead statues by John van Nost mark out the Orangery Terrace

Opposite Deer on the Powis estate – a reminder that this was a medieval deer park

The lure of the landscape

In 1771 the garden again made another leap into contemporary fashion. This was a time when formal gardens throughout Britain were being dug up in favour of more naturalistic landscape parks, of water, trees and green spaces that came right to the door of the mansion.

The great proponent of the landscape movement was Lancelot 'Capability' Brown (1716–83), his work principally confined to England. In Wales, his place was partly filled by William Emes (1730–1803) and as part of improvements to the estate the 1st Earl of Powis (2nd creation) employed Emes to divert the public road where it passed close under the north side of the Castle.

Emes left intact Winde's hanging terraces below the Castle, although he might reasonably have removed them to reveal the magnificent stone crag better suited to the manner of a landscape park. Perhaps Emes's light hand was due to the boldness and high quality of Winde's terraces? Perhaps there would have been too much work involved in removing terraces which in any case made such practical sense of the steep terrain? Whatever the reason, the terraces survived the excessive clearances that typified the landscape movement elsewhere. Emes did however undertake planting on the ridge to the south of the Castle – the Wilderness – which enclosed the terraces and the Dutch water garden, planting many of the fine oaks that survive to this day. Yet another feature of contemporary fashion now lay before the Castle.

But whether gardens thrive or not depends on the interest of their owners at any particular moment, and by 1784 the 2nd Earl had let the terraces go to rack and ruin, in favour of life in London.

Later developments

In the early 1800s, Powis passed first to the son, then the grandson of Robert Clive, the man who brought India into the British Empire, and under their care the garden was returned to 'the most complete and perfect state of repair'.

Informality unfolds

Contemporary perfection required a softer, looser manner throughout the garden. By 1809 the Dutch water garden had been removed in favour of a simple lawn where deer grazed to the bottom of the terraces.

On the lower grassy terraces, small trees and shrubs flourished. On the upper more formal terraces, the once intricately clipped yews were allowed to become informal trees, and the wall-trained fruit trees were removed. Creepers grew up the walls of the Castle. The geometry of the Italianate design was being washed over with naturalistic shapes.

Violet's creation

The garden jogged along through the rest of the 19th century with no major changes, until it found a new enthusiast in the person of Violet (1865–1929), wife of the 4th Earl of Powis. Her great-grandfather had been a Lane-Fox of Bramham Park, Yorkshire, a gardening dynasty that continues to this day. Still in her forties, she persuaded the Earl to let her manage and improve the garden.

There were particular problems pressing: several of the tall elms that formed the fourth, eastern 'wall' around the secret terrace garden had fallen, and the last remaining trees had to be removed with the result that the walled kitchen garden and glasshouses were now in full view from the Castle. And, while the terraces were a grand place for her ambitious flower gardening, they were hardly suitable for large social occasions or children's play.

Left *Violet Lane-Fox, Countess of Powis* by Ellis Roberts

Below left Climbers and small shrubs add informality to this area of the garden

So it was that Violet Powis relocated the entire kitchen garden, glasshouses and all, to a new position behind the Wilderness ridge and on its empty footprint she made a new Formal Garden. The elms were not replaced and the Formal Garden became part of the view from the Castle, yet another layer of contemporary gardening, once again created not over the top but to the side of the older garden.

Violet's Formal Garden was typically Edwardian, comprised of flat open spaces set within walls and hedges, where there was room for prettiness in flower borders and blossoming fruit trees. At the same time Violet set to work enriching the planting on the terraces with new varieties of shrubs and perennials, in her attempt to make Powis 'one of the most beautiful gardens in Wales and England'.

Preservation and beyond

The garden remained unchanged after Violet's death in 1929, until Powis Castle passed into the care of the National Trust in 1952. Since then, the Trust has continued to pursue her ambitions for the garden while preserving its many-layered historic structure, but also finding space for 21st-century gardening, including modern preoccupations with meadow gardening and wildlife.

Above Vivid colours on the Orangery Terrace

Below Looking towards the Formal Garden from the Orangery Terrace

The Garden and the Seasons

Today Powis is unquestionably a garden for all seasons, with something to please the eye even in the crisp days of winter.

Spring bulbs

Spring begins with dwarf bulbs. Sheets of yellow aconites light up the banks of the Formal Garden, followed by grape hyacinths and scillas under apple trees. Primroses flourish on the grassy slopes below the terraces. As the season progresses, thousands of the naturalised wild Welsh daffodils (*Narcissus pseudonarcissus*) bloom in the Paddock.

Summer blooms

As the season warms up, magnolias in all parts of the garden expose their goblet-shaped flowers on bare branches, pink or white against a blue sky. Early summer sees apple blossom and, on walls and trellises, Powis's many wisterias spread their long purple tassels. In the terrace borders the first flush of early perennials is starting to make colour.

What would an English – or indeed a Welsh – garden be without roses? In June they flower in profusion and in all kinds – climbers and bushes, species and hybrids, with pedigrees ancient and modern, some in massed displays, some trained on hoops in the flower borders.

By July the herbaceous borders are a mass of flowers. As the weeks go by, the fashionable tropical planting of the Top Terrace gets into its stride, becoming ever fuller and more flamboyant until the frosts knock it back. In the Formal Garden the ranks of delphiniums give way to a display of towering hollyhocks that must surely outdo those of any other garden.

Above *Penstemon* 'Burgundy', *Malva moschota f. alba* and *Verbascum chaixii* 'Album'

Left Narcissi flower in great swathes in early spring

Autumn shades

September sees the lowest of the terrace borders showing its colours in sedums, asters and tall, deep-blue aconites while, alongside, the maples of the lower slopes begin to turn their striking shades of gold and orange.

Meanwhile the gardeners can be seen beginning the massive task of clipping the huge yew trees and hedges that are such an icon of Powis. To watch them at work, hoisted 14m in the air, is to realise just how challenging a gardener's job can be.

Winter structure

As the leaves fall, the garden takes on its winter guise, in the shapes of topiary and intricately trained fruit trees, sparkling under frost or casting their long shadows in the low afternoon light. This is the time to appreciate the garden's structure and how it has been made.

Above The clean lines of the yew hedging and topiary are sharpened by a winter frost

Left Seedheads are an attractive feature of the garden in autumn

Tour of the Garden

Even today that first view of the garden at Powis is a complete surprise. As you enter through a little woodland gate, head left along the Top Terrace towards the Castle walls and all will be revealed.

The Top Terrace

Powis's deep, raised border is planted for exotic effect. Chusan palms and *Magnolia grandiflora* form an evergreen core, but most of the planting is tender perennials. There is the very un-British, outsized foliage of bananas and the fat, suckering stems of the rice-paper tree, *Tetrapanax papyrifer*.

Above Bananas and cannas add a touch of exoticism to this summer border

A passion for exotics

Of middle size but seeming taller in a raised bed are cannas, fuchsias and abutilons with both loud-coloured foliage and flowers, and the strappy leaves of miscanthus. Tender salvias, scarlet *Lobelia tupa*, *Osteospermum* and heliotropes fill the ground row, accompanied by the succulent rosettes of Canary Island aeoniums. This remarkable showpiece border was developed under the hand of Powis's former head gardener Jimmy Hancock (1972–96), one of the founding fathers of today's fashion for exotics.

The nature of the planting here does not mean that the garden at Powis (and its terraces in particular) has an unusually mild climate, only that, with the reflected heat from the terrace walls and using many warmth-loving plants brought on under glass early in the season, a border such as this can be planted out for the season in early summer and will then reach a dramatic peak as the season ends.

Terrific topiary

Press on along the Top Terrace and pass between some of Powis's 14 massive yew 'tumps' (or in Welsh 'twmpathau yw'); they are William Winde's original topiary pieces, now grown into monumental organic shapes. Perhaps take a moment to pause in the seat which has been carved into the canopy of one of them.

The view unfolds

Finally, you will come to the garden's great moment. There, beyond the low wall and fine lead urns, the entire garden and secret valley is laid out: at your feet, the terraces descending through a pattern of elegant staircases and statues to the Great Lawn (once the water garden); ahead, William Emes's Wilderness ridge and its towering oaks; to the right the Daffodil Paddock; to the left, the crisply hedged spaces of the Edwardian Formal Garden and, beyond it, the deer park and wide valley leading to the pointed profiles of Long Mountain and the Breidden hills.

Three-hundred years of garden-making all there before your eyes, sitting happily and spectacularly together; it is a rare sight. All that is missing is the Dutch water garden and cascade on the Great Lawn, although sometimes, in a nod to the space's lost geometry, temporary summer mowing patterns in the turf amusingly commemorate the events of Powis's past.

Above This lush border in the Top Terrace combines the impressive shrub *Tetrapanax papyrifer* with *Persicaria microphylla* 'Red Dragon', *Salvia* 'Indigo Spires' and penstemons

Left *Penstemon* 'Countess of Dalkeith', *Antirrhinum* 'Cinnamon Spice' and *Salvia patens* 'Guanajuato'

The Top Terrace

The Terrace wall is made of brick, once regarded as more modern and civilised than stone. Its colour matches perfectly the natural reddish-pink stone of the steps and walls of the Castle itself.

In a series of tall Baroque niches once meant for statuary, elegant terracotta vases today provide sophisticated colour throughout the season. Once again, an early season spent under glass means that the vases can be put into place in full, luscious flower. In late summer, cuttings are taken of all the Top Terrace's tender plants so that vigorous young specimens can be ready to plant out the following season.

Silver sensation

Below the niches in poor dry soil runs a line of the low, silver-leaved *Artemisia* 'Powis Castle' which was named by the former head gardener Jimmy Hancock in 1972; it is now planted worldwide in gardens great and small and is a stalwart plant for dry gardens. One of its virtues is that it produces very few flowers (they are insignificant) to spoil the foliage effect. A modest specimen of 'Powis Castle' above the wall is said to be the original plant from which all others worldwide have been propagated.

Above View from the Top Terrace in autumn

Right Huge, billowing yews on the Top Terrace

Yew beauty

Beyond *Hercules* rises one of Powis's best-known monuments, the 14m high English yew hedge (*Taxus baccata*) which forms the boundary of the Top Terrace. Like the yew tumps, it has outgrown its original formal, far smaller outline, to become a vast rollicking cloud formation of dark greenery. It follows the terrace right to its edge, jutting out into space and into the sky like a great wall, before stepping down to the next terrace, now fatter and chunkier, to continue its job of enclosing the terraces and creating a plinth for the Castle itself.

Garden art

At the far end of the Top Terrace is a large open lawn with a sculpture of *Hercules* slaying the many-headed Hydra with his club. It is the work of Andries Carpentière and was made in the Flemish workshops of John van Nost. It once stood in the lost water garden below the terraces, as did *Fame and Pegasus* which now stands in the courtyard before the western Castle entrance.

Look from this lawn up the bare rock cliff and you will see the Castle's original and east-facing main entrance; it was from here in the 18th century that the original surprise view of the garden was to be seen.

Near Hercules is a large clipped drum of the evergreen oak tree, *Quercus ilex*, adding to the variety of colours and textures in the terraces' green monuments and, like an honorary yew tump, a large strawberry tree droops over the steps down to the next terrace.

Above The lead statue of *Hercules* with magnolia in the foreground

Right The view of the yew hedges at the end of the terraces

The Yew Hedges

Left One of the gardeners pruning the yew tumps from a cherry picker

Below The view from the Top Terrace down to the garden below, with the immense yew hedges in the foreground

Overleaf Autumn colours at the western end of the terraces

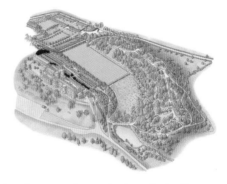

The clipped yew along Powis's terraces – the 14 tumps, the 14m high hedge – remain in the mind long after a visit is over, not only because of their sheer size, but because they are such a major element of the garden. Looking back to the Castle from the Wilderness ridge, you can see how their massive forms provide a visual foundation for the weight of the Castle above, and yet the way they seem to melt over the edges of the terraces, like wax, gives them fluidity, too.

Origins and survival

The work involved in maintaining them is enormous, although today, with modern machinery, it is much reduced. But why are the yews here at all? Would it not have been easier for past generations simply to remove them, when, by weight alone, they put great pressure on the terrace walls?

The answer is probably twofold. The number of yews is only a fraction of the original number and probably represents those retained in the early 19th century to become small trees, when the Castle was given a more informal appearance. Later, at their new size, they were clipped again, perhaps to save the work of their removal and the damage this would do, and also to provide some counterweight to the long, complicated flower borders of the Edwardian

garden. Between the garden's periods of enthusiastic development, there were also times when the garden simply coasted, and coasting – benign neglect – is often the saviour of many a plant, garden and house.

It is not only the Terrace's great hedge and tumps that require clipping. There is a golden yew, added later, a cultivar regularly used as a formal accent in 19th- and 20th-century gardens, which has been tightened by clipping, and there are of course long lengths of box hedging which run along the front of the borders themselves.

Keeping trim

There are almost 8,500 square metres of formal hedging, and the 14 yew tumps and Top Terrace hedge create another 7,000 square metres of clipping. It used to take ten men four months to clip all the box and yew with hand shears, balanced on very long ladders where necessary. Today power shears are used, which reduces the task considerably. It takes two gardeners six weeks to trim the box, and two men 12 weeks to work on the yew. Another gardener spends ten weeks in the air on a hydraulic cherry picker, from which it is possible to enhance the attractive bulges of the tumps and hedge, while still keeping them under long-term control. The cherry picker itself, which can reach over 14m, is craned onto the Aviary Terrace every year.

The Aviary Terrace

The Aviary Terrace was the first one in its day to have a formal entertaining space at its centre. We should imagine this terrace as it was originally, with long gravel paths stretching away on each side, lined with fruit trees and topiary, along which to stroll in conversation and look down upon the ornate water garden.

Under Violet Powis, the Aviary Terrace was planted with hybrid musk roses so popular and new at that time. Today, since the soil is unsuitably dry, it contains plants that can cope with baking sun and drought, although old magnolias thrive against the wall.

There are many Mediterranean-climate plants which enjoy ground that is dry in summer, including Jerusalem sage, oily-leaved cistus, salvias and euphorbias. Leathery evergreen foliage comes from olearias and spiky leaves from *Astelia chathamica* and *Eryngium pandanifolium*. The colour scheme is warmer on the west side and paler on the east, the kind of contrast which is found on all the terraces, for the sake of variety.

Tender plants

The Aviary itself sits tucked into the cliff under the Top Terrace, its line of arches draped with Japanese wisteria. It is no longer used to keep birds but instead is enclosed by temporary polythene frames in the worst winter weather, to allow the cultivation of tender rhododendrons, fragrant in early

Stately statues

Dancing along the balustrade in front of the Aviary is a line of statues, of life-size shepherds and shepherdesses happily playing pipes and apparently admiring the view of the garden. Once again they were made in the Flemish van Nost workshop and are now beautifully restored (lead statuary slumps upon its internal steel frame with age) to show off their complex curls and draperies and sheer *joie de vivre*.

Today we see them as our fashion prefers, the colour of weathered lead, but during the early 18th century they may have been painted in bright colours – blues, yellows and flesh tones – to make them lifelike and jolly; this was certainly fashionable at the time. They are a telling reminder that these terraces were meant to be a place of delight as well as a statement of fashion and power.

spring; the name 'Fragrantissimum' could not be more appropriate. With them, fronds of the chain fern, *Woodwardia radicans*, arch out approximately 1.5m, ready to root at the tip and form a chain as they do outdoors in favoured Cornish gardens.

As in many an Italian garden building, the interior walls and roof of the Aviary are clad in the creeping evergreen fig, *Ficus pumila*, so different from its sisters the edible fig and the indoor rubber plant. It roots as it goes, like ivy, making small, thumbnail-sized leaves. Then when it encounters open space it makes bushier, flowering growth with far larger foliage.

Above Detail from one of the lead statues

Left The Aviary Terrace

Right The statues on the terrace represent shepherds and shepherdesses

The Orangery Terrace

Right Looking towards
Orangery Terrace, with
Rosa 'Buff Beauty' and
phlox in the foreground

Below Summer flowers
on the terrace

Here you can fully appreciate what these terraces were about: a touch of Italy in Wales. Like the Aviary above it, the Orangery is tucked into the cliff, making the terrace over 20m deep, a remarkable feat on such a steep site. This was the central entertaining space where one could circulate in company, dine and enjoy the sight and the sound of the Water Garden and cascade below.

Behind the elegant sash windows of the Orangery, potted citrus trees are still kept through the cold months and brought out in summer, leaving the interior decorated with orange- and yellow-trumpeted clivias. Tight shapes of holly and box set upon lawns echo more formally the giant tumps above, and against the Orangery wall climbers such as the pale yellow Banksian rose rise behind neat box

hedges. The grand, 18th-century classical stone doorway was brought here from the west end of the Castle itself by Violet Powis, when she and her husband were returning the Castle to its more medieval appearance.

Inspired borders

Either side of the Orangery run pairs of parallel borders, made successful because the imported soil is deep and rich. These were the creation of Violet Powis, an admirer of that great gardener and writer, Gertrude Jekyll, but in their present form they were inspired by plans drawn up in the 1970s by the National Trust's first Gardens Adviser, Graham Stuart Thomas, a great late 20th-century gardener and writer, and by succeeding advisers.

Set behind long box hedges, the borders are at their best from high summer to early

autumn, densely planted and with never a gap of bare soil. This is no mean feat when you consider that they have to be seen from the terrace above as well as close up. At the back of the borders are wall shrubs and climbers including clematis and ceanothus. A conifer rises up 6m to make a winter accent, and roses are carefully trained on to splendid hoop formations at the centre of the borders.

A profusion of perennials

The main feature of the borders, however, are the perennials, cooler coloured at the east end, hotter at the west end. On the cool side are grey-and-white *Crambe cordifolia* and *Chelone obliqua*, and the drooping swan-necks of *Lysimachia clethroides*. On the hot side are rich reds found in crocosmias, and dahlias 'Grenadier' and 'Bishop of Llandaff'. There are the brassy plates of *Achillea filipendulina* 'Cloth of Gold' and massed ochre shades of *Helenium* 'Moerheim Beauty' and *H.* 'Sahin's Early Flowerer', and hundreds more.

Final descent

If it were 1700 today, you would now descend from the Orangery by a grand central staircase through the lower grass banks to the Water Garden below, but since its removal in the early 19th century the Orangery Terrace has marked the end to high formality. However, you can still descend again through yet more stairs, to the last, more informal Lower Terrace, for a last breath of colour.

The Lower Terrace
The Box Walk

The Lower Terrace

Gone, here, is the rigid geometry of the upper terraces, the statuary, the buildings and the topiary. The Lower Terrace may be just as long, but it slopes gently and informally from end to end to absorb the irregularities of the land.

Against the terrace wall is a border designed to keep colour going after the Orangery Terrace borders quieten down in mid-autumn. Japanese anemones are a great stalwart – 'Honorine Jobert' and 'September Charm' – as are the tall sedums and asters. Rose hips glow red and shrubby fuchsias and indigofera flower right into the first winter frosts.

Trees and shrubs

On the other side of the path, there were once clean grassy banks stepping down to the Water Garden, later planted in the 19th century with small, informal trees and later still with apple trees (the area is now known as the Apple Slope).

Today it contains an early 20th-century collection of small ornamental trees and shrubs, scattered across the slopes. It includes maples, dogwoods and smoke bushes (*Cotinus*), which provide rich leaf colour in the autumn, good to appreciate from this terrace as the low sun shines through them, but also spectacular when seen *en masse* from the opposite Wilderness ridge. They form the podium upon which the terraces and Castle sit. Under the trees are massed bulbs for spring and autumn; daffodils and primroses in April, with ox-eye daisies in the long grass in summer.

The Box Walk

Up to this point, the garden has been all horizontal terraces and grand stairs, all complex planting and long, outward views – the 17th-century core of Powis. Now comes a complete change.

The Box Walk is a link between the terraces and the Edwardian Formal Garden, and for a complete change of mood there is a slope underfoot, a narrow path wide enough for one person, winding its way downwards between hedges. There are no flowers to engage the attention, just simple greenery and the strange, loved-or-loathed odour of box. But what box! On the low side is a chunky, waist-high hedge that acts as a balustrade, but on the other uphill side it rises to 4m, not as billowing as the great 14m yew hedge above, but gently folding along in abstract planes, a compromise between the great hedge and the razor-edge geometry of the smaller hedges coming up in the Formal Garden.

Above The Box Walk

Left *Cotinus*, or smoke bush, in autumn

Opposite Steps down to the Lower Terrace

The Formal Garden

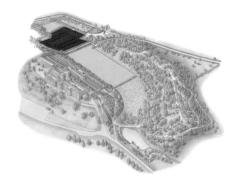

Violet Powis had great ambitions for her garden in 1911. With the towering elms below the terraces lost to old age and storms, the kitchen garden was exposed to view from the windows of the Castle and she felt it must be removed to make way for her new Formal Garden.

Hers was a polite yet romantic manner of gardening which the 17th-century terraces had never really provided, even in their earliest days of gravel walks and wall-trained fruit trees. The mechanical, behind-the-scenes kitchen garden was now completely out of sight, vineries and all, and the entire garden at Powis was hers to develop and improve according to prevailing good taste. Putting firmly in its place the state of the garden as she had found it on first coming to live at Powis, she declared confidently:

'It grieves me that the garden itself should be so far below, instead of above, the average. It will not be my fault if I fail [to improve it]. It will not be from lack of energy or of taste. But I must really work myself as I see the failure which results from leaving the care of the garden entirely to the gardeners.'

Violet Powis

Right Looking towards the Formal Garden and the countryside beyond

Below The vine arch

Opposite The original gardeners' bothy is now let as a National Trust holiday cottage

The Formal Garden today

So, today, the Box Walk delivers you into the Formal Garden past bulb-scattered banks of maples, smoke bushes and magnolias, to open lawns, wide gravel paths and flat land at last, where there is space for people and parties and children. There is a sense of relaxation which cannot be achieved on hanging terraces so dominated by the towering Castle walls. As if to prove a point, straight ahead now is a pale bench comfortably wrapped in a great arch of box. A large but very domestic gardeners' bothy (now a holiday cottage – The Bothy) looks on, keeping order.

There is a love of discipline in the Formal Garden and it begins at once with avenues of carefully trained apples and pears, of period varieties such as *Malus* 'Broad-Eyed Pippin' and *M.* 'American Mother'. Underneath them, with Edwardian precision, are neatly edged beds of carpet planting: lamb's ears, lamium and golden marjoram, interplanted with grape hyacinths and scillas. It is the gardening of children's story books.

On a cross axis to the apple avenues is a vine arch, low-topped and just right for children, and honeysuckles romp over a row of oak posts. The axis ends in another pale seat, this time bowered in clipped yew, from where you can enjoy a long border of modern English roses. If the structure and geometry of the terraces are of stone walls and steps, here they are made from living plants.

The Croquet Lawn
The Fountain Garden

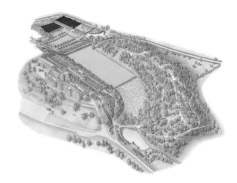

The Croquet Lawn

Near the Bothy is a croquet lawn which still occasionally resounds to the tock of mallet on wood. Croquet took England by storm in the 1860s, only to be eclipsed by tennis in the following decade, but it grew again in popularity in the 1890s and found its place here at Powis.

Here, too, is to be seen one of Powis's show-stopping horticultural moments. Backed by a tall wall, there is a long border filled with a June display of delphiniums such as you may well see nowhere else today, and in August, when gardens are supposed to be lacking in colour, it is filled with hollyhocks, many of them towering way above the wall. It is this kind of cottage gardening on a grand scale that typified the Formal Garden as a whole.

Such concentrated displays of plants are always difficult to pull off and highly bred plants can be martyrs to disease, but at Powis the hollyhocks are grown to perfection through painstaking attention to their health and vigour. Opposite the hollyhocks is another equally long border, this time planted with many tall, hardy fuchsias, taking colour on into the autumn.

Opposite Detail of the Bodley Gate showing the Powis coat of arms, which combines the elephant of the Clives and the griffin of the Herberts

Below left Magnolia in bloom

Below right Erythronium in the garden in spring

The Fountain Garden

With the Dutch water garden long gone and no water on the terraces, it is perhaps not surprising that Lady Violet should have made a generous fountain in her new Formal Garden. It stands in open lawn, a round stone basin with grass to its very lip and a jet shooting into the air from a shallow vase at its centre.

Down the sides of the lawn stand parallel mounds of clipped yew, crisply rounded in profile and firmly anchored upon the ground, in complete contrast to the sagging tumps of the terraces.

Around the Fountain Garden are narrow raised beds at the foot of the enclosing yew hedges, containing sprawling plants to soften the perimeter of the garden. Small mounds are made by varieties of *Potentilla fruticosa* and *Aster turbinellus*, while the ivy, *Hedera* 'Angularis Aurea', billows cheerfully along the western side.

A gravel path runs through the Formal Garden to a wrought-iron gate, a gift from Lady Violet to her husband. It is a copy by the architect G. F. Bodley of the early 18th-century gate shown in a print of Powis House, the family's London home which was demolished in the 20th century. That path and the gate are the link to the relocated kitchen garden.

Moving west up a bank of steps, the path now passes through a cool green corridor of yew, another of the garden's quiet moments between show-pieces, to reach the Wilderness.

Right Backlit water in the Fountain Garden

The Wilderness

The wooded ridge opposite the castle, known as the Wilderness or Pleasure Ground, is a small fold in the landscape which hides the terraced garden from the great sweep of the valley beyond. Looking back from the far side of the valley the Castle stands out pink against the hills, but the garden is invisible.

At the centre of the Wilderness's north side, facing the Castle, is a steep *allée* of grass ending in a stone vase. It was here that the cascade once fell down to the Dutch water garden on the Great Lawn below. Today you can still imagine how impressive those terraces must have been, lined with crisp topiary and geometrically trained fruit trees. There is the Castle, sitting up above the Aviary and Orangery and tall retaining walls, a brooding Italian palazzo to its complex terraces. Yet to see the full scope of the terraces you must stand right on the edge of Great Lawn itself and appreciate, at last, their sheer width and the scale of the yew tumps and massive hedge. This is perhaps the most iconic image of all Welsh gardens.

Right Looking towards the Wilderness from the terraces

Opposite The Wilderness

But the Wilderness has other, smaller pleasures to offer. Nearby under the trees, on a low path, stands a mossy Plunge Bath surrounded by ferns, where in the 19th century the family could take invigorating cold baths, as was the fashion. The ridge also bears a contemporary stamp in the form of a sculpture by Vincent Woropay (1952–2002) which was installed here in 1987; it is a colossal stone foot, typical of Woropay's monumental forms.

Looking south from the top of the ridge, you can see across to the river plain and countryside of the Welsh–English border lands, once so vigorously contested by Powis's early owners.

A collection of trees

The Wilderness ridge was carefully planted with trees when William Emes worked on the estate in the 1770s and you can walk beneath his great oaks to this day. Their trunks have been consistently cleaned of their lower branches from an early age to make smooth, towering boles that belie their 230 years.

In the years after Emes's planting, the ridge was fenced off and added to the garden again, so that exotic new trees could be introduced: conifers such as the Californian redwoods (*Sequoia sempervirens*), great firs and the American tulip tree, *Liriodendron tulipifera*. Later additions include the handkerchief tree, *Davidia involucrata*, southern beech (*Nothofagus*), Japanese cedar (*Cryptomeria japonica*), white-barked birches, and small groves of the suckering angelica tree, *Aralia elata*, known for its stems studded with short, vicious spines.

The 19th century also saw the introduction of rhododendrons and azaleas. Seedlings of the plain purple *Rhododendron ponticum* are being rooted out in favour of the more colourful named varieties and, when space then appears, new generations of trees can be planted against the day when Emes's oaks pass maturity.

The Daffodil Paddock and Western Bank
The Stable Pond and Ice House

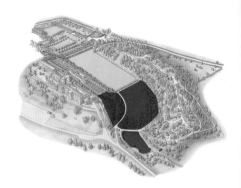

The Daffodil Paddock and Western Bank

Below the Wilderness and separated from the Great Lawn by a yew hedge, is an area known as the Daffodil Paddock. In the 1700s scheme this space was a lozenge-shaped formal garden of complex geometric paths centred on a pool. The pool is no surprise since this area and the adjacent Great Lawn stand upon an underground water course. Both spaces have always been wet land.

The lozenge garden was removed along with the water garden in the early 19th century, so what else could be done with this boggy space? The answer has been to turn it over to a more modern way of gardening, in the form of a meadow, here studded with the wild Welsh daffodils (*Narcissus pseudonarcissus*) which have naturalised successfully. There are sheets of the more common wildflowers such as primroses and buttercups, but also wild orchids and yellow rattle which so successfully inhibits the growth of grasses allowing the wildflowers to dominate. Notice the strange, convoluted trunk of the bog-loving dawn redwood tree, *Metasequoia*, only discovered as recently as the 1940s.

The paddock is allowed to grow unchecked until the flowers have set seed; in August when hopefully the land is at its driest, the meadow is mown and the hay removed, after which it quickly turns green again and is mown as a coarse lawn for the rest of the season.

At the head of the paddock where the land rises to a pool beyond, moisture-loving shrubs such as dogwood and bamboo thrive. On the adjacent Western Bank, there is a fine group of *Eucryphia* 'Nymansay', like a pillar of white roses in August, and a large, peeling, coppery, paperbark maple, *Acer griseum*.

Right **The Stable Pond**

Opposite **Naturalised Welsh daffodils in spring**

Below left **New leaves emerging from the maple,** *Acer pseudoplatanus* **'Brilliantissimum'**

The Stable Pond and Ice House

Beyond the Daffodil Paddock lies a small pond, looking out to the edge of the deer park. It is the garden's one natural water body, adding greatly to the variety of habitats for wildlife.

Its banks are planted with rushes, great woody mounds of the royal fern *Osmunda regalis*, and the coarse, outsized leaves and huge flower heads of *Gunnera manicata*, from Brazil. On the far bank is a fine, multi-stemmed example of a curious form of the Japanese cedar known as *Cryptomeria japonica* 'Elegans', grown for its feathery foliage and unique, burnished-bronze winter colour.

Tucked under the trees on the Wilderness side of the pond is a subterranean Ice House, once carefully packed in winter with ice collected from the pond and preserved for summer use in the kitchens, to chill drinks and produce luxuries such as ice cream. Around it stand some of Powis's, and indeed Britain's, largest and finest angelica trees.

As you head back towards the Castle, you will pass the fan-shaped foliage of a ginkgo tree, a plant which once grew in Britain in prehistoric times, making Powis's 300 years seem no more than a blink in the eye of nature. But still, what a memorable blink it is.

The Garden Today

All gardens, even historic gardens, are living entities, which develop over the years according to the effects of time, climate, interest and money. The garden at Powis has seen some hard times as well as good, but today it is doing splendidly.

Its several historic styles have miraculously survived and stand as examples to be studied and enjoyed by all. Its planting is the envy of gardeners worldwide and the skills of its gardeners are famous; many managers and head gardeners of Britain's most important gardens were once apprentices at Powis.

But Powis is working for the future, too. Behind the scenes, Violet's kitchen garden has become the nursery, the powerhouse of today's garden. In her well-maintained original glasshouses, thousands of plants are reared for the garden and for sale to visitors. All this is achieved on a carbon-neutral basis, taking heat for the greenhouses from ground-source pumps and from photo-voltaic panels. The nursery's water supply is drawn from a bore-hole and supplied to plants grown in peat-free compost. Every scrap of green waste from the garden is composted and, as in centuries past, the gardeners still go into the woods in winter to cut hazel twigs and poles for use as supports in the herbaceous borders.

Throughout the site, whether in design, planting or practice, the old sits happily and productively with the new – surely a recipe for success in any garden.

Below Visitor with a dahlia grown in the nursery at Powis